China Briefing

The Practical Application of China Business

For further volumes:
http://www.springer.com/series/8839
http://www.asiabriefingmedia.com

Dezan Shira & Associates is a specialist foreign direct investment practice, providing business advisory, tax, accounting, payroll and due diligence services to multinationals investing in China, Hong Kong, India and Vietnam. Established in 1992, the firm is a leading regional practice in Asia with seventeen offices in four jurisdictions, employing over 170 business advisory and tax professionals.

We also provide useful business information through our media and publishing house, Asia Briefing.

Chris Devonshire-Ellis · Andy Scott ·
Sam Woollard
Editors

Setting Up Representative Offices in China

Fourth Edition

 Springer   **DEZAN SHIRA & ASSOCIATES**

Editors
Chris Devonshire-Ellis
Andy Scott
Sam Woollard
Dezan Shira & Associates
Asia Briefing Ltd.
Unit 1618, 16/F., Miramar Tower
132 Nathan Road
Tsim Sha Tsui, Kowloon
Hong Kong, People's Republic of China
e-mail: editor@asiabriefingmedia.com

ISBN 978-3-642-16070-7   e-ISBN 978-3-642-16071-4
DOI 10.1007/978-3-642-16071-4

Springer Heidelberg Dordrecht London New York

Published by Springer-Verlag Berlin Heidelberg
© Asia Briefing Ltd. 2008, 2011

This work is subject to copyright. All rights are reserved, whether the whole or part of the material is concerned, specifically the rights of translation, reprinting, reuse of illustrations, recitation, broadcasting, reproduction on microfilm or in any other way, and storage in data banks. Duplication of this publication or parts thereof is permitted only under the provisions of the German Copyright Law of September 9, 1965, in its current version, and permission for use must always be obtained from Springer. Violations are liable to prosecution under the German Copyright Law.

The use of general descriptive names, registered names, trademarks, etc. in this publication does not imply, even in the absence of a specific statement, that such names are exempt from the relevant protective laws and regulations and therefore free for general use.

Cover design: eStudio Calamar, Berlin/Figueres

Printed on acid-free paper

Springer is part of Springer Science+Business Media (www.springer.com)

About China Briefing's China Business Guides

Thank you for buying this book. China Briefing's publications are designed to fill a niche in the provision of information about business law and tax in China. When we decided, several years ago, to commence this series, we did so in the knowledge that much that was available about China was either expensive, or completely contradictory. Plus much of it did not really adequately address the real issues faced by businessmen—the practical knowledge that must be part of any business dealings in developing countries. This guide is designed to change that perspective and provide detailed information and the regulatory background to business in China—but with a firm eye also on the details of making money and remaining in compliance.

Accordingly, we have made this guide informative, easy to read and inexpensive. To do so we have engaged not a team of journalists or academics—but the services of a respected professional services firm to assist us. The articles and materials within have been researched and written by China-based Chinese and international accountants and auditors, familiar with the issues that foreign invested enterprises face in China—as they service them in China as clients. These professionals have come from the nationally established practice, Dezan Shira & Associates, and we are grateful for their support. Without them this book would not have been possible, and we wholeheartedly recommend their services should you require sensible and pragmatic advice as contained within this book.

At China Briefing, our motto is "The practical application of China business" and we hope that within this volume and our other publications you feel we have achieved this, and helped point you in the right direction when it comes to understanding and researching this vast and complicated business environment.

Asia Briefing Publications
Hong Kong

Contents

Establishing Representative Offices 1

Staffing the Organization. 9

Tax and Financial Issues 27

Other Issues 37

Glossary of Terms. 43

Establishing Representative Offices

1 Application Procedures and Flow Chart

Representative Offices (ROs) are useful and relatively inexpensive vehicles for establishing a presence in China. However, they can be complicated to set up so here we explain the mechanisms to do so.

Some of the benefits and advantages of having a representative office include the fact that there is no capital requirement to be operational, and that you can set up an entity in China even on a shoe-string budget by just paying office rental, utilities and salaries. Compared with the investment required for other forms of foreign-invested enterprise (FIE), the expenses to set up an RO are substantially lower and you would be able to carry out liaison activities between your headquarters and clients/potential clients or suppliers in China. Market research, supplier identifications and quality checks can also be conducted out of ROs, as well as any other preparatory work on behalf of the holding company.

An RO allows foreign business people to obtain important and legally required working visas and residence permits, as well as legally employ local staff. It paves the way for more extended and substantial investments by the headquarters in the future. ROs have also been very popular entry-vehicles in China for international traders buying local goods for export and for firms wishing to sell foreign goods domestically.

However, every coin has two sides. According to relevant regulations, an RO cannot engage in direct business activities. For example, they may not negotiate and conclude contracts or issue invoices for services or sales in China directly. As a result, it can be considered a cost-centre only financed on a regular basis by the holding company. Any income derived from business transactions is not allowed to go through the RO local bank account.

On November 19, 2010, the Chinese State Council issued the *Regulations on the Administration of Resident Representative Offices of Foreign Enterprises* (RO Administrative Regulations), which took effect on March 1, 2011, replacing the previous regulations that have been in force since 1983.

Article 13 of the Regulations specifically provide that ROs cannot engage in any profit activities except for those activities which China has agreed on in international agreements or treaties.

Article 14 further specifies that the activities ROs can be involved in include

(i) market research, display and publicity activities that relate to company products or services; as well as
(ii) liaison activities that relate to company product sales or provision of services, and domestic procurement and investment.

ROs will be subject to penalties of RMB 50,000 to RMB 500,000 for each profit activity as well as confiscation of the illegal income and relevant assets for conducting such activities, and RMB 10,000 to RMB 100,000 for exceeding the permitted business scope mentioned above.

Basic Requirements for Setting Up a Representative Office in the PRC

The State Administration of Industry and Commerce (SAIC) issued the Notice on Further Strengthening the Registration and Administration of Permanent Representative Offices of Foreign Enterprises on January 4, 2010, which had substantial effect on foreign investors setting up representative offices in China, as well as ROs already established on the mainland. The circular stipulate the following:

- The parent company must have been in existence for two years.
- In addition to the incorporation certificate, a bank reference letter will also will need to be notarized and legalized.
- The registration certificate for an RO is now only valid for one year rather than three years; all existing ROs will have a one-year valid registration license when they renew their current registration certificate.
- Every year when an RO renews its license, a notarized and legalized incorporation certificate of the parent company will need to be provided.
- Foreign representatives of an RO, including the chief representative, cannot exceed four; for existing ROs with more than four foreign representatives (including a chief representative), the AIC will not require the RO to decrease their number of representatives but will not approve any additional foreign representatives.

- The local branch of the AIC will verify all the information of the RO including its registered address within three months after the RO obtains its registration certificate.

In February 2011, the SAIC issued the Circular on the Thorough Implementation of the RO Administrative Regulations, which provides that an RO can decide its own duration as long as it falls within the duration of its parent office. Further, all ROs shall have the same business scope as follows: "engage in non-profit making business activities related to its parent office."

Procedures for Setting Up a Representative Office in the PRC

1. Acquire preliminary approval at the relevant governing authority. Before May 2004, foreign companies engaging in advertising, pharmaceutical, trade, manufacturing, freight forwarding, contracting, consulting, investing, leasing, educating, and railway transportation were required to get approval from the competent local bureau of the Ministry of Commerce. This procedure has now been simplified and the preliminary approval requirement has been cancelled. However, ROs of foreign companies involved in some specific industries still involve approvals from other authorities specifically supervising an industry. For example, the China Banking Regulatory Commission shall oversee foreign banking enterprises and financial institutions branches in the PRC.
2. Register with the Administration of Industry and Commerce to get the "Registration Certificate for Representative Office of Foreign (Hong Kong, Macao and Taiwan) Enterprises."
3. Apply for carving the official chops (RO chop and financial chop), and register with the Public Security Bureau.
4. Apply at the Bureau of Quality and Technology Supervision for the Enterprise Code.
5. Apply for Local Tax Registration.
6. Apply for State Tax Registration.
7. Register at the State Administration of Foreign Exchange if a foreign currency account is needed.
8. Open bank accounts (basic RMB account and foreign exchange current account).
9. Enter into employment contract with the designated departments under the labor bureau, or with FESCO or other licensed HR agencies.

Documents Required (Please Note that There May Be Regional Variations)

1. Valid Incorporation Certificate and/or Business Registration Certificate of holding company indicating that it has been in existence for no less than 2 years.

2. Bank reference letter elaborating basic information about the applicant (name, legal address, date of opening of the account, registered capital, borrowing facility (credit standing) and overall comments made by the bank), issued by a financial institution that has a business relationship with the company.
3. Identity certificate (ID card, passport copy and visa, or other valid identity certificate) of the chief representative.
4. Articles of Association of the holding company.
5. Letter appointing the authorized signatory of the holding company.
6. Letter appointing the chief representative and other representatives.

Items 1–6 need to be notarized by a local public notary in the investor home country and legalized by the Chinese embassy/consulate responsible for the investor jurisdiction.

7. Official office/premises lease or purchase contract together with the landlord property certificate (Please note there are some regional variations. See next page for more details).
8. Resume of the chief representative with his or her signature.
9. Photo of the chief representative.

If the documents are in a foreign language, then a Chinese translation by an eligible translation company is required.

The Administrative Regulations require ROs to submit an annual report between March 1 and June 30 every year providing information on the legal status and standing information of the foreign enterprise, ongoing business activities of the RO, and payment balance audited by their accounting agencies. The registration authorities will issue fines if the RO fails to provide such reports on time or provide false information.

Tax Implications

According to relevant tax laws, rules and regulations, ROs are required to pay Business Tax (BT), Corporate Income Tax (CIT), Value-Added Tax (VAT), Individual Income Tax (IIT), and Stamp Duties. Business Tax and IIT shall be reported monthly while CIT shall be reported quarterly in most cities. If the chief representative is a foreign national, whether they stay in China or not, they shall be subject to individual tax based on the income derived from the RO. This is addressed in more detail in the later tax section.

Issues to Consider During RO Applications

- Ensure all permits and licenses are renewed on time and give yourself enough notice to start renewal procedures (30 days in advance is necessary).

- Generally speaking, residential units do not have the licenses to allow RO registrations.
- When it comes to selecting the right office space make sure that the building itself or the owner of the office have the right certificates allowing you to register the RO with the local authorities.
- The term of the lease agreement shall be no less than 1 year and the office must be located in a Grade A building.
- If either the tenant or the landlord is of non-PRC nationality, the lease agreement needs to be signed in front of a notary public officer. However, be aware of regional differences. For example, in Beijing, foreign individuals cannot qualify as a landlord—this is connected to the government's recent move to limit foreign individuals or foreign companies from purchasing real estate in the domestic market. The only exception being that the parent company purchases an office for the use of its RO in China.
- The restrictions imposed on Hong Kong, Macao, and Taiwan are different from the restrictions for foreign nationals.
- As you would require official invoices from the landlord (in case of rental), please ensure that this requirement is clearly addressed during price negotiations and they are responsible for related tax issues—in fact, it may happen that the landlord will pass their own tax dues over to you.
- Local tax officers are increasingly suspicious of low monthly declared salaries for foreign chief representatives in China, so ensure the real amount is reported to the local authorities.
- The widespread practice of using separate private accounts to fund ROs activities in order to reduce the official RO monthly tax liability is illegal and cross-checks are on the rise.

2 RO Applications—Common Mistakes

Applying for an RO is a complex process and some China consultants do not advise their clients about everything that is required. Equally, clients may make mistakes during the application process. Here we list some of the more common errors.

Office Premises—General

When arranging office premises, ensure the landlord has a certificate giving him permission to rent to foreign entities. This document is a requirement of all RO applications and without it your application cannot proceed. However, this also places the landlord in a higher tax bracket, so many do not obtain the required certificate. If you sign a contract and pay a deposit without ensuring the documents are all in place, you may lose the deposit as well as lose time on the application.

Setting up a Representative Office

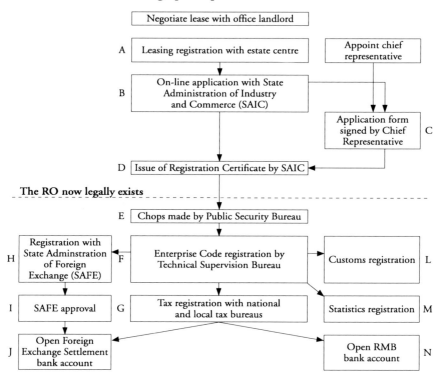

Procedures for Chief Representative personal permits

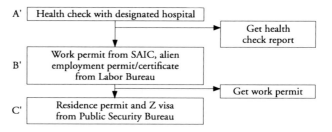

Notes - there are some regional variations to this process
1. *Shenzhen - SAFE registration/approval not required*
2. *Guangzhou - lease agreement does not need to be notarized; customs registration usually not required; foreign exchange account not required*
3. *Beijing - only commercial buildings can be used as registration address; some minor differences to registration of leasing agreement*

Most (but not all cities) require that the office is in a Grade A building. This certificate is issued by the Ministry of Commerce, and a copy is required as part of the application. Fortunately, most cities now have a large number (and varying qualities) of Grade A buildings, so it is not as much of a choice or cost problem as in the past.

Make doubly sure you have the following documents:

- Premises Ownership Certificate—this needs to be provided by the landlord and with the company seal.
- Landlord's Business License—this is also required with the company seal.
- RO Resident's Certificate—issued by the building management company.

Office Premises—Shanghai

Shanghai has recently been developing more, and not less, official bureaucracy and administration—somewhat out of step with its purported international image. These new regulations have also mainly been issued without prior warning and at great inconvenience to applicants with pending licenses.

Notably, all RO applications now require the regional lease record certificate, which has to be obtained from the real estate authority. An original copy needs to be provided to the local tax bureau and the Administration of Industry & Commerce.

Shanghai's "Government Agents" Process

Shanghai is also unique in that all applications for all registration certificates must go via government agents. This adds another layer of cost and administration. It also means applications are effectively taken out of the hands of professional services firms and can be held up if for example a smaller or cheaper agent is used, and then goes on holiday or is just lazy or overworked! Larger professional services firms tend to obtain better results when dealing with Shanghai's government agents due to the volume of business. Cheaper does not mean better service in Shanghai (or anywhere else in China for that matter).

Bank Accounts

Many clients authorize their agent to open the bank account, although in reality they can do this themselves. However, in order to avoid any inconvenience, the agent often simply opens the bank account without asking the clients how to manage the account. If the agent is a friend of the local employee assisting you there can be a conflict of interest here, as there are security issues that need to be discussed before opening the bank account, such as:

- Whether to use chops (company seals) to manage the bank account in addition to signatures (we recommend this as it places an additional layer of security)?
- Whose signature and chops will be used for account management?
- Whether other signatories can manage the account with differing responsibilities, and if so who?

Many agents will just open the account with the accounting chop and chief representative chop, without checking the security or desired wishes concerning the above issues with the holding company. It is quite dangerous for clients to wire their registered capital into such an account, of which the clients know nothing, and cases of money disappearing or being skimmed off have unfortunately been far too common.

Staffing the Organization

1 General Issues

A Representative Office (RO) employing local staff must apply to a foreign service entity designated by the local government for engaging such employees. A related contract must be entered into between the RO and the foreign service entity.

With an extensive branch network in major Chinese cities, the Foreign Enterprise Service Corporation (FESCO) is the most well known provider of HR related services to ROs in China. It is interesting to note that in recent years many similar organizations have been mushrooming in open competition with FESCO—do your homework in assessing whether these new players have been officially approved and their business scope includes HR management and related services.

Even though ROs will conduct their own hiring activities through recruitment ads, interviews, etc., they are prohibited from hiring Chinese employees, whether directly or indirectly through other organizations, and must entrust above-mentioned units (such as FESCO, China International Intellectual Corporation, China International Talent Development Center, etc.) to do this.

Typically, an RO will sign a "contract for service" agreement with the local service unit. Under such contracts the local service unit agree to provide, and the ROs agree to pay for, employee hiring services and for administering the employment relationship.

Once the RO has decided on a candidate, the local service unit will sign an employment contract with the employee.

The local service unit will handle on a regular basis the employee's mandatory contributions for unemployment insurance, medical insurance, housing and retirement. The local service unit also administers the employee's personal file, obtains residence or temporary residence permits, and obtains a passport or visa for the employees whenever required. Finally, it initiates, renews and terminates employment contracts with the employees. ROs must pay FESCO fees for these services, which vary according to different locations.

The RO will usually sign, again with the tacit approval of the local service unit, a supplemental employment contract with the employee that may provide for detailed rights and obligations of the employee (for example, based on the company HR policy). It is commonly understood that the supplemental contract may not come into conflict with the primary service contract between the RO and the local service unit. Supplemental provisions typically include details of compensation, holidays, work duties, office rules and regulations, confidentiality, etc.

We have included a sample labor contract so you can see the sort of issues that must be covered. Our comments are in boxes in the text and the notes at the end. Note that the details may vary from city to city.

Company Code:

.... Human Resource Agency Co., Ltd.

and

Its Employee Dispatched

Labor Contract

Approved by .... Labor Bureau

Party A (the company)
Name: .... Human Resource Agency Co., Ltd.
Type: Limited Liability Company
Address: ....
Post Code: _____
Legal representative: _____
Contact person: _____
Tel No.: _____
Party B (employee)
Name: _____
Gender: _____ Age: _____
ID No.: _____
Address: _____
Post Code: _____
Tel No.: _____

    Based on the principles of equality, voluntariness and after friendly negotiations, the two parties concerned have concluded this Contract according to the stipulations of the *Labor Law of People's Republic of China*, the *Labor Contract Law* and the *Labor Contract Ordinance of*................................. *Zone*, as follows:

I. Position

    With the entrustment of the receiving company _____, Party A will employ Party B, and dispatch Party B to work for the receiving company. Party B's exact position would be decided by _____.

    The receiving company has the right to adjust Party B's position according to its actual needs.

II. Term of the contract (including trial period)

  1. Term

    Party A and Party B agrees that the Term of this Contract would be fixed as the _____ th item below:

    (1) A fixed period of _____ year(s), the contract would be valid from _____ to _____.

    (2) Unfixed period. The contract would be effective from _____.[1]

    (3) The period is fixed according to the specific job. The contract would be valid from _____ to the date until the job is finished.

---

[1] According to the *Labor Contact Law*, Party A or the receiving Company and Party B may conclude an unfixed-term employment contract upon reaching a consensus based on negotiation. If Party B proposes or agrees to renew his employment contract or to conclude an employment contract in any of the following circumstance, an unfixed-term employment contract shall be concluded, unless Party A requires the conclusion of a fixed-term employment contract: (1) Party B has been working for the receiving Company for a consecutive period of no less than 10 years. (2) Prior to the renewal, a fixed-term employment contract was concluded on two consecutive occasions.

2. Trial period
   (1) No trial period
   (2) The trial period is _____ month(s) (the trial period is included in the Term).[2]

   Assessment and assessment standards in the trial period would be decided by the receiving company. If Party B does not meet the requirements of the receiving company, then it would be deemed that Party B does not meet the requirements of Party A, and Party A will have the right to cancel the Contract according to Article 39 of the *Labor Contract Law*.

III. Work schedules (time)

Party B's receiving company will implement one of the work schedules below[3]:

1. Standard work schedule of 8 h a day and 40 h a week;
2. Unfixed work schedule;
3. Comprehensive work schedule.

> The receiving company could prolong the work hours after negotiating and agreeing with Party B on condition that it is necessary due to the requirements of the company's operation. However, overtime could not be more than one hour per day. If there were some special reasons for further prolonging work time, then overtime could not go beyond three hours per day under the conditions of ensuring Party B's health. Under no circumstances should the total overtime in a month exceed 36 hours.
>
> If any prolonging of work hours occurred by reason of some other situations stipulated in law or administrative regulations, then it would not be subject to the restrictions of the above stipulations.

IV. Salary and treatment
   1. Salary in the trial period would be RMB _____/month. Salary after the trial period would be RMB _____/month. Salary would be given by Party A directly.

---

[2] If an employment contract has a term of not less than 3 months but less than 1 year, the probation period may not exceed 1 month; if an employment contract has a term of more than 1 year and less than 3 years, the probation period may not exceed 2 months; and if an employment contract has a term of not less than 3 years or is unfixed, the probation period may not exceed 6 months.

[3] If the receiving company could not implement the standard work schedule system, but implement the unfixed work time system or comprehensive work time system due to its job nature or operational character, then it should be approved by the authorities in charge.

2. The receiving company would pay the salary in _____ or in _____ every month.
3. Payment for overtime would be paid by the receiving company according to Article 44 of the *Labor Law*.

> Under PRC law, an employer may extend his/her working hours if such extension is "necessary for production and operation." Any such extension should not exceed 3 hours per day or 36 h per month and the employer is liable to pay additional remuneration as follows:
>
> - on working days—not less than 150% of the hourly wage;
> - on rest days—not less than 200% of the hourly wage;
> - on statutory holidays—not less than 300% of the hourly wage.

4. In a period of illness or non-occupational injury, the salary policy would comply with the *Salary Management Interim Provision for Enterprises in .... Zone* and other laws or regulations.
5. Salary should be paid regularly if Party B fulfilled his or her work duties required by laws in his or her work time.
6. Salary policy of downtime should comply with the *Salary Management Interim Provision for Enterprises in .... Zone* and other laws or regulations.
7. Party B has the right to enjoy vacation according to laws or regulations concerned. Salary policy for vacation will comply with the regulations of central or local government.

> Holidays: notwithstanding anything to the contrary contained in the employment contract, under PRC law, an employee is entitled to take a total of 10 days statutory leave on National Holidays (i.e. New Year, Spring Festival, Tomb Sweeping Day, Labor Day, Dragon Boat Festival, Mid-Autumn Festival and National Day). Pursuant to *Ordinance of Paid Annual Leave of Employees*, if the employee has served one full year but less than 10 years in total in the receiving company, he is entitled to a minimum 5 days of annual leave. If he has served 10 full years but less than 20 years, minimum annual leave is 10 days. If he has served for 20 full years, minimum annual leave is 20 days.

8. Any breach of the contract caused by the receiving company should be reported to Party A within 1 month after Party B is aware of such a breach.

V. Labor protection and labor condition

1. Party A shall urge the receiving company to provide Party B a safe and healthy working condition, as well as necessary labor protection equipment required by relating regulations and laws. If Party B works in an

environment with occupational hazards, the receiving company shall give Party B regular health inspections.
2. Party B has the right to refuse to carry out a job involving great risk, and has the right to file a complaint against the receiving company if it disregards the safety and health of its employees.

VI. Social insurance and welfare
1. Party A shall handle the social insurance matters for Party B according to relevant regulations issued by .... government.
2. Party B's occupational injury and death should be handled in accordance with *Occupational Injury and Insurance Ordinance of* .... *Zone*.
3. Party A shall make best efforts to improve Party B's welfare.

VII. Labor discipline
Party B shall meet requirements as follows:
1. Comply with all regulations of the receiving company.
2. Strictly abide by safe operational procedures to ensure safe production.
3. Complete the assignments given by the receiving company in a timely manner.
4. Keep the receiving company or Party A's business secret.
5. Comply with the population policy issued by the central or local government.
The company rules of the receiving company would be deemed as Party A's company rules. If Party B was dismissed by the receiving company labor discipline as a result of breaching then it would be regarded to have breached Party A's company rules. In this case, Party A has the right to terminate the Contract according to law and stipulations in the Contract.

VIII. Modification, cancellation, re-signing and termination of the Contract
If any situation stipulated in the Contract for modifying, canceling, re-signing and terminating the contract occurred while Party B was working in the receiving company, then it would be deemed that the condition for modifying, canceling, re-signing and terminating the Contract emerged. Consequently, the two parties concerned have the right to invoke requirements for modifying, canceling, re-signing and terminating the contract according to stipulations, as well as the right to claim related compensation or reimbursement.
1. The two parties could modify the contract according to laws. The modified Contract would become effective after being signed or stamped by the two parties (if the original Contract needed to be verified, then it should be verified by authorities concerned).
2. Party A has the right to cancel the Contract at any time if any of the following matters occurred:

(1) Party B turns out to not meet the requirements of the receiving company during the trial period.
(2) Party B commits serious breach of the regulations of the receiving company.
(3) Party B has grossly neglected his or her duty, committed self-seeking misconduct, or caused serious damage to Party A or the receiving company.
(4) Party B has additionally established an employment relationship with another employer which materially affects the completion of his tasks with the receiving Company, or he refuses to rectify the matter after the same is brought to his attention by the receiving company.
(5) Party B has violated criminal law.
(6) Other matters forbidden by laws or regulations have occurred.

3. Party A has the right to cancel the labor contract, however it should be done with written notice to Party B 30 days in advance, if any of the following situations occur:

(1) If any of the following circumstances makes it necessary to reduce the workforce by 20 persons or more or by a number of persons that is less than 20 but accounts for 10 percent or more of the total number of the enterprise's employees, the employer may reduce the workforce after it has explained the circumstance to its labor union or to all of its employees 30 days in advance, has considered the opinions of the labor union or the employees and has subsequently reported the workforce reduction plan to the labor administration department:

  (a) restructuring pursuant to the Enterprise Bankruptcy Law;
  (b) serious difficulties in production and/or business operations;
  (c) the enterprise switches production, introduces a major technological innovation or revises its business method, and, after amendment of employment contracts, still needs to reduce its workforce;
  (d) another major change in the objective economic circumstances relied upon at the time of conclusion of the employment contract, rendering it unperformable.

(2) Party B developed illness or suffered non-occupational injury, and could not perform the original job or another job arranged by Party A after rehabilitation.
(3) Party B was not qualified to perform the job, even after training or adjustment in position.
(4) The original contract could not be fulfilled due to the fact that the objective situation, which is foundation of the contract, has

significantly changed. Meanwhile, the two parties could not reach a new agreement.

4. Party A may not dissolve the contract according to Clause 3 of this article, if any of the situations below occur:

    (1) Party B is engaged in operations exposing him to occupational disease hazards and has not undergone a pre-departure occupational health check-up, or is suspected of having contracted an occupational disease and is being diagnosed or under medical observation.
    (2) Party B developed an occupational disease or received occupational injury, and has been confirmed that he or she has partially or totally lost labor ability.
    (3) Party B developed an occupational disease or received occupational injury and is still in the healing period.
    (4) Party B is in the period of pregnancy, birth or breast feeding.
    (5) Party B has been working for the Employer continuously for not less than 15 years and is less than 5 years away from his legal retirement age.
    (6) Other situations stipulated by laws or regulations.

5. Party B has the right to inform Party A of the dissolution of the labor contract under the conditions below:

    (1) The receiving company has not fulfilled the salary payment on time or has not provided the proper labor conditions or labor protection.
    (2) The receiving company fails to pay the social insurance for Party B in accordance with the law.
    (3) The receiving company has rules and regulations that violate laws or regulations, thereby harming the worker's rights and interests.
    (4) Other situations stipulated in laws or regulations.
    If the receiving company or Party A uses violence, threats or unlawful restriction of personal freedom to compel Party B to work, or if Party B is instructed in violation of rules and regulations or peremptorily ordered by the receiving company or Party A to perform dangerous operations which threaten his personal safety, Party B may terminate his employment contract forthwith without giving prior notice to the receiving company or Party A.

6. The labor contract would be automatically dissolved if any of the conditions below emerged:

    (1) The Term expires.
    (2) Party B has commenced drawing his basic old age insurance pension in accordance with the law.
    (3) The receiving company is declared bankrupt through legal procedure.
    (4) The receiving company was dissolved by laws.
    (5) Party B's death.

1 General Issues   17

(6) Other situations regulated in laws or regulations.
(7) If Party B wants to cancel the contract, he or she should inform Party A 30 days in advance, or 3 days in advance during his or her trial period, except under the situation that are covered by Clause 5 of this article.
(8) Re-signing labor contract.

After the Contract's expiry day, if the two parties intend to continue the labor relationship (e.g. Party B intend to continue his or her work in the receiving company and the receiving company intend to continue to employ Party B), the Contract should be re-signed within 30 days ahead of the expiry day.

IX. Liabilities for breach

1. Party A's legal liabilities
   (1) If the receiving company pays Party B's salary in arrears or embezzles Party B's salary, or refuses to pay Party B's overtime payment, then Party A shall pay the money in full to Party B. In addition, Party A shall give Party B an additional sum amounting to 25% of Party B's salary as compensation.
   (2) If the receiving company's salary is lower than the minimum salary, then Party A shall pay the difference to Party B. In addition, Party A shall give Party B an additional 1% of the difference as compensation.
   (3) Any economic loss incurred by Party B as a result of Party A's failure to fulfill the obligations stipulated in Clause 1 of Article VI should be assumed by Party A according to the relevant regulations issued by the local government.
   (4) Party A shall pay one-off compensation to Party B if any of the following situations occur[4]:
       (a) Party B dissolves the Contract according to Clause 5, Article VIII of the Contract.
       (b) Party A dissolves the Contract and the two parties concerned reached an agreement on the dissolution.
       (c) Party A dissolve the contract according to Clause 3, Article VIII of the Contract.
       (d) The employment contract is a fixed-term contract and has expired, except in the situation where Party B does not agree to renew the contract even though the conditions offered by the

---

[4] Compensation standard should be computed according to Party B's working seniority in the receiving company. If he or she had worked in the company for over 1 year, then amount of compensation would be equal to a monthly salary (it is the same case if the working time is over 6 months and less than 1 year). The monthly salary means average monthly salary of the 3 months before dissolving the contract. If the contract was dissolved according to item 3 of Clause 3, Article VIII and item 4 (a) of Clause 1, Article IX, then the maximum compensation can not exceed the amount of 12 month's salary.

receiving company or Party A are the same as or better than those stipulated in the current contract.

(e) The Contract ends pursuant to Items (1) and (2) of Clause 6, Article VIII.

(f) Other situations stipulated in laws or regulations.

(5) Party A dissolves the Contract according to Item 2 of Clause 3, Article VIII. In addition, Party A shall also pay one-off medical allowance to Party B according to the relevant regulations.

(6) Party A dissolves the contract according to Items 2–4 of Clause 3, Article VIII. If Party A failed to informed Party B 30 days in advance, then Party A shall compensate Party B an additional 1 month's salary.

2. Party B's legal liabilities

If Party A or the receiving company suffers economic loss due to Party B's violation or dissolution of the Contract, then Party B shall compensate Party A the following items:

(1) The professional training expense Party A has assumed.
(2) Direct economic loss suffered by the receiving company.

3. Additional liabilities for breach are as follows:

_____
_____

X. Dispute resolution

If any disputes rise from the three parties concerned, Party A shall negotiate with the receiving company. If negotiation fails or Party B does not agree with the resolution, then Party B could apply arbitration for Labor Arbitration Committee. If the parties concerned agree with the arbitration, then it should be implemented. Otherwise, any party could institute legal proceedings with the people's court.

XI. The contract would become effective from the day of signing or stamping.

XII. The contract is in duplicate. Each party shall hold one copy.

XIII. The following documents[5] are affixes of the contract. They have the same legal validity as the contract.

Stamp of Party A
Legal Representative's signature:
Signature of Party B
Contract signing
Date:
Stamp of Verification authority (if applicable)
Date:

---

[5] Any changes to the contract shall be made in accordance with the laws and regulations. Otherwise, it would have no legal effect.

2 Dismissing Chinese Employees

There are strict rules governing the termination of staff in China, especially if the employee is either pregnant, suffering from work-related injury or is receiving medical care.

Let us look at a few instances that commonly occur.

Probation (or Trial) Period

During this period Party A or the receiving company may terminate the engagement with immediate notice. For Party B, he or she can terminate the contract by giving 3 days notice.

Automatic Termination

If employment contracts are of a specific term, then upon expiry of the contract, the employee's position is automatically terminated without recourse. Some labor bureaus and organisations like FESCO do have fixed term contracts for Chinese staff, so these can be used if required to see out contracts for unsatisfactory personnel without incurring penalties. Please review your contracts with such agencies beforehand to ensure you are not committed to any more than this.

Termination with Notice and Compensation

Provided a 30 day notice period is given, the employer may terminate an employment contract under the following circumstances:

(a) the employee is incapable of fulfilling their duties due to non-work related injury or illness after completion of medical treatment;
(b) the employee is incapable of fulfilling his/her duties, and continues to be incapable of fulfilling them after training or being assigned to a different position;
(c) there is a material change in the circumstances based on which the employment contract was entered into, such that the contract can no longer be performed, and no agreement on contractual modifications can be reached.

Summary Dismissal

An employer may terminate employment contracts without notice under the following circumstances:
(a) the employee is proved during the probation period to not meet the qualifications for employment;
(b) the employee seriously violates the labor disciplines and the rules and regulations of the company;
(c) the employee causes loss to the company due to serious dereliction of duties or engagement in malpractice for selfish ends;
(d) the employee is convicted of a criminal offence.

Compensation Issues

This is defined as being 1 month's salary for every full year of service but no more than 12 months' salary.

Penalty Clauses

These are commonly used, and although an employment contract may specify that an employee, if leaving within a certain period, may be liable for repayment of certain defined expenses such as professional training, re-location costs and so on, penalty clauses requiring the employee to repay a sum of money upon resignation are generally void and may be challenged.

3 Expatriate Individual Income Tax in China

Individual Income Tax (IIT)

There has unfortunately been a lot of nonsense spoken about registering for individual income tax in China, how much to pay, being paid partially overseas, actually working here but consistently on tourist visas and so on. The real picture over registering, assessing liabilities and paying IIT in China has become rather muddled. Ask one expatriate, then ask another, and they will give you different opinions. However unfortunately, expatriates do not decide China's tax regulations. Neither is the situation short of clarity in the eyes of China's tax bureau, who are quite clear on the subject and who are progressively clamping down on abuse of non-working visas and the under-declaration of income by foreigners in China.

Here we outline the circumstances, liabilities and procedures for registering for Individual Income Tax (IIT), explain the rationale and hope to take some of the pain away from being a tax payer in the PRC. Assessment of IIT can be very complex—if you have concerns, take good professional advice. You should also do your homework well in advance to assess your personal tax situation with the related authorities and ensure you are in compliance—China's tax authorities are increasingly targeting expatriates who evade or only partially declare their IIT, with painful consequences for them and the international companies who employ them if tax is found to have been under declared.

Tracking Liabilities

Up until recently, China has been able to effectively track potential tax abuse only by inspecting foreigner's passports and crosschecking with the tax bureau over whether or not registration had been completed. In practice such inter-government bureau co-operation never really transpired, with the Immigration and Tax Bureau worlds apart. This has now changed and more information-sharing activities are taking place between different bureaus in the country. Entry/exit forms are computerized with the data compiled and made available to the tax bureau who now, at a glance, can ascertain visa types, length of stay, numbers of entries/exits and other information to assess whether IIT is applicable or not. This means that the Chinese authorities can effectively track movements of aliens through the country and retrieve data pertinent to tax assessments, as is common in most Western nations. New regulations have also specified how to count the days in China, specifically the arrival date and departure date. These will all be counted as days effectively spent in China and are actively used for computation of IIT purposes.

"Self Reporting" Individual Income Tax rules

At the beginning of November 2006, the State Administration of Taxation (SAT) released the *Trial Individual Income Tax Self Reporting Regulation*, Guo Shui Fa (2006) 162 (Circular 162). This stipulates that individuals with a yearly income of over RMB120,000 shall "self report" their income tax together with other personal information within 3 months of the end of the tax year.

This follows an amendment made on October 27, 2005 to Article 8 of the *Individual Income Tax Law*, stating that "individuals with an income exceeding the amount set by the State Council" shall self-report their income and pay taxes thus incurred. The State Council set this threshold at RMB120,000 and authorized SAT to make a detailed regulation on the matter, which they have now done.

Individuals should file the tax "self report" if they have:

- personal income that exceeds RMB120,000;
- two income sources within China;
- income derived from outside China;
- taxable income but without specific taxpayers designated (i.e. taxable income but no withholding agent such as an employer);
- other cases where the State Council thinks they should pay income taxes.

There are a few limited exceptions. Individuals staying in China "less than one full year" will not be affected by items 1 or 3 above. To qualify, they must be absent for more than 30 consecutive days or more than 90 cumulative days in the relevant calendar year.

Eleven types of taxable income are included when assessing whether an individual has annual income of more than RMB120,000. They are:

- income from wages and salaries;
- income from production and business operations by industrial or commercial households;
- income from remuneration for labor services;
- income from remuneration for manuscripts;
- income from royalties;
- income from interest or dividends;
- income from the leasing of property;
- income from sales of property;
- contingent income;
- other kinds of income specified as taxable by the relevant authorities.

There does remain some uncertainty about whether expatriates who have lived in China for more than one year but less than five full years are required to report non-employment income from overseas such as investment or property incomes, and further clarification on these issues may be needed from SAT. However, some categories of income appear to be excluded—notably, in terms of expatriates, for example income sourced from outside China by an individual who has stayed in China for more than 1 year but less than five full years.

Taxpayers with annual incomes of more than RMB120,000 should complete an annual tax return as well as their routine monthly tax filing, whether via their employer or individually. This annual return should be finished before the end of March each year (the Chinese tax year is the same as the calendar year). However, it should be noted that individuals who have income from outside China should make their annual reporting within 30 days i.e. by January 30 every year. Meanwhile, those with salary or wages from two or more sources within China but who do not have a withholding agent are required to self report within 7 days of the end of the month, i.e. by January 7.

This system makes the IIT mechanism similar to that for Corporate Income Tax, which requires monthly and annual returns. It also gives the tax bureau a "reconciliation" role to ensure that monthly returns by employers can be matched with what the individuals themselves report.

In addition, for expatriate staff, company accountants had often been responsible for making IIT filings without the direct involvement of the foreign employee. By insisting on this declaration from the foreigner directly, the responsibility is passed onto the foreigner—there is no way out. And, if the two filings do not balance then tax authorities can easily identify false declarations.

But overall, the policy intention would appear to be to provide an additional check that high earning individuals—domestic and foreign—have paid all their tax, some of which may be on income that is not simply from a single employer. It also brings the Chinese system, at least for such taxpayers, into line with the likes of, for example, the USA and UK systems.

Who Has to Pay?

China has a multi-tiered system of tax liabilities for foreigners, which has led to some confusion, particularly over the so-called "90 or 183 days rule." We identify the more likely scenarios and the tax liabilities as follows.

Expatriates on Extended Business Trips to China

If you are sent by your organization to China and your salary is paid off-shore (probably in your home country) and you spend more than 183 days in China in a calendar year, then you have to pay IIT in China based on the days you effectively spend in the country. This means that if you spend in China, let us say, 184 days within a calendar year, than you would have to pay taxes on all income sourced from China (meaning income related to your work performed in China).

Foreigners Working for Legal Enterprises in China

Without going into too many complicated calculations, if you hold positions such as the Chief Representative (CR) of a Representative Office (RO) or the General Manager of a Chinese Limited Company, Wholly Foreign-Owned Enterprise or a Joint Venture anywhere in China, then you are subject to IIT from the first day you commence work in the country. Interestingly, should you not actually visit China within a calendar year but are still acting as the Chief Representative of a Representative Office, then zero tax filings should *still* be made monthly to the local authorities. Some locations (such as Shenzhen) may not require this.

According to the law you should declare the full salary for the position and pay IIT accordingly. In practice, however, it is common to see foreigners declaring an "arranged" fixed salary for their China position (with the rest being paid off-shore) and pay taxes accordingly, lowering to a great extent their full tax liability. This practice is *illegal*, so be careful should you decide to pursue this route. While this has been common practice in the past, it also puts the employer out of compliance—fines of several million RMB have been levied just recently to FIEs engaged in such practices in China. The risk of being caught, with the issue now highlighted at audit, is increasing.

Foreigners Holding Concurrent Posts Both in China and Elsewhere

Firstly, you should be arriving in China on a business visa, and are subject to IIT based on the number of physical days you are in China. This is assessed upon the total salary you are claiming from your local employment position and from the parent company overseas—the Chinese tax bureau may want to see proof of earnings from your parent company (tax slip, payment voucher etc.) to support your case. At the end of each month, your China office should take copies of your passport, together with the entry/exit stamps for that month, and file and pay for taxes based upon the number of days spent in the PRC. The tax bureau will issue a receipt showing this has been paid, and this can be credited against the tax paid in your resident location (i.e. you would not have to pay tax both in China and your resident location for the time spent in China).

China Residency Status and IIT on Your Worldwide Income

Be aware that if you are regarded as a tax resident by the Chinese government, which means you have stayed in China for more than 5 years (without residing outside the PRC for more than 90 days cumulatively each calendar year or 30 consecutive days always within a calendar year), you have to pay IIT on your worldwide income without limitation of source. This means that shall you have income elsewhere related to property rentals or interests, these shall also be declared to the Chinese tax authorities. The taxes paid overseas can be deducted from the taxes payable to the Chinese tax authorities. To be fair, we did ask the State Administration of Tax if they had ever collected such revenues, and the honest (and slightly bashful) answer was "No"—however why expose yourself to such a law without reason? It is easy to avoid so count those days and give yourself a month out of China every 5 years.

Work Permit Registration Procedures

If you are based in China and working here, then you should apply for a working visa, working permit and residence card.

Please be aware that constant checks in residential areas are conducted by the local Public Security Bureau. One of the first things you should do when you arrive and rent an apartment in the country (if you check in at a local hotel you will be given a form to fill out with your details) is to get registered with the local *Pai Chu Suo* (local police responsible for your area). You should register yourself even if you are not planning to take up an official position in China and only decide to "live" there.

Before you obtain all the documents mentioned above you should also go through a medical examination at the appointed local hospital. It should not take you more than a couple of hours to get through the exams with the results normally being issued the day after (or if you pay more on the same day!). Your spouse and children (if any) would also have to register with the local authorities.

Expatriate Tax Rates and Liabilities

The first RMB4,800 of the expat's monthly income in China is tax free. That does not mean you can rush out and declare salaries of RMB5,000! The tax bureaus are wise to this and will demand to see concrete proof of your earnings elsewhere. If you cannot provide this, they may refuse to register you, immediately making your presence in China illegal.

China's IIT rates are high compared to neighboring countries. The following table demonstrates salary brackets and tax rates, plus the quick tax deduction system. Your total liability can be calculated as follows:

Salary minus 4,800 × tax rate, less quick deduction figure = IIT tax bill

Monthly taxable salary	Tax rate (%)	Quick calculation deduction
<RMB500	5	RMB0
≥RMB500 and <RMB 2,000	10	RMB25
≥RMB2,000 and <RMB5,000	15	RMB125
≥RMB5,000 and <RMB20,000	20	RMB375
≥RMB20,001 and <RMB40,000	25	RMB1,375
≥RMB40,001 and <RMB60,000	30	RMB3,375
≥RMB60,001 and <RMB80,000	35	RMB6,375
≥RMB80,001 and <RMB100,000	40	RMB10,375
≥RMB100,000	45	RMB15,375

There are some implicit or explicit benchmarks at local tax bureaus on what a reasonable salary is in certain industries and this could vary with your position, your education background and your home country. Local authorities have the power to increase your declared salary. Should this be manifestly low or inadequate to your position, they shall assume and obtain the proved confirmation that you are deliberately reducing the figure to escape from a higher IIT threshold. This can be enormously damaging for you and your employer who would be placed under far greater tax scrutiny in the future for potential tax evasion issues within the business.

Deductible Allowances

China is also pretty reasonable regarding non-taxable elements as part of an expat package, however some attention may need to be paid to the structuring of the inclusive package with certain items needing to be properly defined in the employment contract.

As a rule of thumb, if you pay for the expenses yourself (against local official invoices) and the company provides you cash allowances, then these are considered taxable. On the other hand, if the company pays for certain expenses on your behalf (e.g. your apartment rental), then this kind of allowance may be exempt from tax and can be deducted from your company CIT computation basis. However, whether or not these expenses are tax-exemptible is ultimately subject to the tax officer's judgment.

Provisional Examples of Benefits

Housing, meal and laundry allowances
Relocation expenses
Travel allowance
Home trip allowance
Language training
Children education allowance
Social security benefits

Enterprises are obligated to withhold employees' IIT when paying salaries to them; failing to do so will cause penalties. Meanwhile, the enterprises can get 2% of the IIT withheld from the tax bureau as commission or handling charge. Pay attention to the calculation of the IIT if the companies are paying IIT for the employees, in this case the income has to be grossed up for the purpose of calculating IIT.

Individual Income Tax calculations for standard salaries are fairly easy to assess, but get more intricate according to the complexity of the expatriate's salary package. It makes sense to take professional advice when structuring expatriate salary packages to ensure liabilities can be planned and catered for in the most tax-efficient manner.

Tax and Financial Issues

1 Tax Filing Obligations for Foreign Businesses in China

So you are looking at setting up shop in the PRC, and need to know exactly what tax liabilities you will face. There is a lot to think about—regional differences for example, as well as uninformed so-called "China experts" muddying the waters. Here, we explain the real situation as regards to tax filing responsibilities in China—how much, when, and what you have to do to get registered and in compliance.

Tax Registration

This must take place as soon as your business license is issued normally within a month from obtaining the business license. Basically, your business license needs to be presented to the local tax office for registration—a separate "tax registrationcertificate" will be issued. It is a serious offence not to have registered for tax withhefty fines being levied for non-compliance, so please ensure this is done. Even if you have tax breaks and holidays pending for your new operations, you must still register.

Tax Liabilities

Guoshuifa [2010] No. 18, issued on February 20, 2010, explicitly stipulates that ROs shall pay corporate income tax on their taxable income, as well as business tax and VAT. Representative offices should perform the principles of actual functions in matching with potential risks, and accurately calculate their taxable income – declaring to the tax authorities at least 15 days after the end of the quarter.

Representative offices that cannot determine their profits on an actual basis must ascertain their deemed tax value by either using the cost-plus method or the actual revenue deemed profit method. Under either method, the new tax circular states that the deemed profit margin shall be no less than 15 percent, an increase from the previous deemed profit margin of 10 percent.

Actual basis method

Representative offices should file taxes on an actual basis, based on books and records, with reported profits in line with the function of the RO.

Calculation:

CIT = Actual taxable profit × CIT rate

BT/VAT = Actual taxable revenue × applicable BT/VAT rate

Cost-plus method

This method is for representative offices that are able to accurately ascertain expenses but not revenue or cost.

Calculation:

CIT = Deemed gross revenue × deemed profit rate × CIT rate

BT = Deemed gross revenue × applicable BT rate

Actual revenue deemed profit method

This method is for representative offices that are able to accurately ascertain revenue but not cost or expenses.

Calculation:

CIT = Actual gross revenue × deemed profit rate × CIT rate

BT/VAT = Taxable revenue × applicable BT/VAT rate

An RO that files taxes using cost-plus or actual revenue methods may, after filing with the in-charge tax authority, switch to the actual basis provided that it can maintain complete accounting books, and accurately calculate its taxable revenue and profit and calculate its tax liabilities.

Some ROs may be able to acquire non-CIT status by invoking treaty protection after completing the relevant filing procedures as stipulated in Guoshuifa [2009] No. 124.

For staff, your local Chinese staff will have their individual income tax and welfare payments catered for by FESCO or a similar organisation—they handle all this for you. FESCO may even pay your staff directly to their individual account every month if so agreed. Alternatively, you internally or your local consultant/agent can do the job. So no problem there—it is all done for you (allow about 40–60% of the basic wage to cater for this location dependent; in some locations you can bargain a reduced fixed service fee too!).

1 Tax Filing Obligations for Foreign Businesses in China

Type of tax	Normal filing procedure	Regional differences
Expat IIT	Filed monthly	Zero payment filing is not required in Shenzhen
Local staff IIT	Filed monthly	Zero payment filing is not required in Shenzhen
Business Tax	Filed monthly in some locations, quarterly in others	In Shanghai, Business Tax and Corporate Income Tax are filed quarterly together in Shanghai. Normally the tax bureau just requires a tax declaration form for BT and CIT, although some require quarterly expenses reports as well
		Beijing requires quarterly filing for business tax
		In South China, monthly filing is required both in Dongguan and Shenzhen while quarterly filing is required in Guangzhou
CIT	Filed annually, although quarterly in some circumstances	See above for situation in Shanghai

Foreign staff must register for Individual Income Tax if they are employed directly by the RO, with their tax filings are normally filed monthly along with the RO tax liabilities. Expat tax liabilities, including rates against salaries, were explained in the previous section of this book so please check there for applicable rates.

2 Annual Audit Requirements for Representative Offices

Under current legislation, all Foreign Invested Enterprises (FIE) such as Foreign-Owned Enterprises, Joint Ventures, and ROs, must be audited on an annual basis.

The deadline for the filing of annual audits is by the end of May of the following year (i.e., your 2010 audited accounts must be filed at the latest by May 2011).

Annual audit of FIE statutory accounts must be conducted by a firm of Certified Public Accountants registered in the PRC under PRC regulations. Previously, only local Chinese CPA firms were permitted to perform the audit function, and international accounting firms were not allowed to enter the Chinese audit field directly. Since 1992 international accounting firms were given permission to establish JV accounting firms with local practitioners.

Key Areas of Annual Audits

When a CPA firm performs an annual audit, in deciding on the appropriate audit procedures for the balance sheet accounts, the auditor should assess the risk of error and fraud in those accounts. What are the key areas they are most concerned about? Obviously in an RO the checks will be carried out in respect of costings rather than revenues. These shall not be understated and official invoices shall be provided as supporting documents. Please consider that all expenses related to the RO shall be declared including even the renovation costs (if any) paid at the beginning of the office lease.

Annual Audit Preparation

Conducting a sound internal review prior to the annual audit is a good idea. The key documents and questions you need to be prepared for are described below. All these issues need to be addressed during your RO annual audit. Please have all the following documents available for the auditors before they arrive—accounting vouchers, account books, financial statements, tax filing records, bank statements, and other related document and reports.

- Cash
    - Bank statement correct?
    - Bank reconciliation correct?
    - Any discrepancies in petty cash?
- Foreign currency issues
    - Is the transaction rate entered correctly? (bear in mind China's July 2005 US$/RMB revaluation and subsequent currency movements)
- Fixed assets
    - FA purchasing—has it been recorded into expenses? If not, has it been approved by the tax authority?
    - FA disposal gain/loss—is it recorded into expenses?
- Funds from the parent company
    - Are these consistent with the parent company's records?
- Interest income/expenses
    - Have they been properly identified in the expenses report?
- Expatriate individual income tax
    - For high level management such as the chief representative, has the IIT calculation been done properly, with correct rate?
    - IIT withholding by RO—has this been completed properly?
- Audit fees
    - Have the audit fees been accrued and separately entered?
    - Are they listed in the expenses report?

- Rental expenses
  - Have these been accrued and entered separately?
  - Are they listed in the expenses report?
- Employer contributions to overseas social security plans?
  - If any employees are involved in such plans, has the payment been recorded into the expenses report?
- Expenses paid on behalf of the head office
  - The expenses may be required to be recorded in the expenses report—this needs to be confirmed with your tax authority
- BT and CIT payments
  - These tax payments should be *excluded* from the expenses report
- Stamp duty
  - Is the RO subject to stamp duty?
- Unofficial invoices (fa piao)
  - Did the RO receive any unofficial invoices? If so, this can be subject to tax penalties
- Business licenses and related administrative matters
  - Is the annual renewal of all of your licenses such as registration certificate, tax licenses, etc. up to date?
- Local employees registered with FESCO and valid work permits for expatriate staff
  - Have these processes been completed in accordance with the pertinent regulations?

  There is a lot to check—if necessary, seek professional advice!

Audit Methods

As previously addressed, all ROs should be audited by a Chinese CPA each year.

Because an ROs taxable income is determined by one of three methods—the cost-plus method, the actual basis method, and the actual revenue deemed income method—these different areas will be monitored by the auditors for the purposes of adjusting the taxable income of the RO as follows.

The Cost-Plus Method

The cost-plus method is popularly used to calculate the deemed taxable income. All expenses incurred by or related to the representative office must be included in the office expenses to calculate the deemed taxable revenue (deemed taxable revenue = office expenses/85%). The expenses include the rental, transportation, telephone, salary, office purchases, entertainment, etc., regardless of whether they are paid from the RO or directly from its head office. Foreign companies often put forward questions such as "If the office rental or salary of the expatriate is paid by the head office, should they be recorded as the expenses of the RO?" Undoubtedly, they are the expenses of the RO. Another notable point concerns salaries paid to resident chief representatives—instead of paying part offshore and part in China, the entire salary of the chief representative or representative should be included in the representative office's expenses, regardless whether they have traveled to China.

The Actual Basis

Detailed contracts signed between the head office and its affiliate company showing the commission rate or detailed service fee amounts and other documents should be provided to the auditors. The auditors will also investigate any undisclosed transactions to determine if there is further taxable income.

The Actual Revenue Deemed Income Method

All the contracts relating to the agency services performed in China should be provided. If the income/commission is not stated in the contracts, a deemed income commission rate would apply.

Based on the adjustment of the taxable income in the audit report, the annual Business Tax and Corporate Income Tax filing should be completed within five months after the end of the tax year. The Chinese tax year is a calendar year, i.e., from January 1 to December 31. Please note in the event of delinquent annual CIT and BT filing and payment, a surcharge for overdue tax payment equivalent to 0.05% per day on the overdue taxes will be imposed.

After the tax authorities review the audit report and the annual filing returns, the tax authorities will issue a notice that either the RO should pay additional tax, that it is correct in its calculations or that it is entitled to tax refunds.

In the process of annual audit, the auditors not only pay attention to the corporate taxes, i.e., BT and CIT, but also other tax issues such as Individual Income Tax and Stamp Duty, etc. These amounts may on occasion only be small—but significant penalties (up to five times the amount due) await the unwary or naïve. It pays to ensure you are in compliance.

Choosing an Auditor

Most small to medium FIEs prefer having accounts audited by a reputable accounting firm with international standards, while at the same time, cost and benefits are also issues to consider.

In addition, in view of the complexity of the China tax regulations, it is recommended that foreign investors should keep themselves abreast of any new rules and the constant changes to these regulations. Your accounting firm should demonstrate a commitment and depth of knowledge to you as well as showing they are capable of understanding international business.

3 Costs and Risks in Under-declaring Staff Salaries and Taxes for Representative Offices

It is a widespread practice for ROs whose activities are taxed through actual and deemed-income methods to receive offshore part if not the majority of the service income (this practice is, however, illegal!), and thus avoid declaring huge amount of revenues in the PRC subject to the local enterprise income tax rate of up to 25%. Without doubt, it is hard for the Chinese government to locate hidden funds outside China, even more so if the holding company/ies are structured in a tax haven or use nominee shareholders. Still the Chinese government has the authority to track your ultimate shareholders and ask for explanations or penalties in the worse cases.

Many ROs would use the cost-plus assessment method for tax and it is thus immediately apparent the fact that if you spend (or officially declare) less then you will end up paying less taxes in the end. From a pure mathematical point of view this is actually true, however, other factors can bring potential dangers to the foreign organization. Here is a list of the most common ones.

1. These malpractices are common everywhere in the country. Chinese authorities are more and more aware of this and it may happen that local withdrawals above a certain amount need to be supported by declarations and signatures at the related bank.

	Wrongdoing	Source of potential danger	Penalties
1	Set up local personal accounts in China under the name of the chief representative to fund RO related expenses not officially booked into the RO a/c to reduce tax liability	Grudged local personnel aware of these arrangements. Chief representative "falling out" with employer	Late payment fines of up to five times the amount of any undeclared taxes that are due, incarceration of chief representative until paid

(continued)

(continued)

	Wrongdoing	Source of potential danger	Penalties
		Competitors Bank and SAFE cross checks	
2	Set up of local personal accounts in China under the name of a Chinese staff to fund RO related expenses not officially booked into the RO a/c to reduce tax liability	Grudged local personnel aware of these arrangements Local personnel leaving the organization for your competitor Bank and SAFE cross checks	As above
3	Withdraw money through local ATMs from foreign accounts to fund RO related expenses not officially booked into the RO a/c to reduce tax liability	As 2	As above
4	Under-declare salaries for expatriates	As 1 Tax bureau cross checks	As above, deportation
5	Not register foreign staff working in the RO	As 2 Public Security Bureau and local police cross checks	As above, deportation
6	Under-declare salaries for local staff	As 1 and 2	As 1
7	Maintain the same declared salary level for both local and expatriates over the years without increase	As 1 and 2 Tax Bureau cross checks	Government imposed audit to check all books, penalties as above if found out of compliance
8	Not register or under-declare the number of local staff	As 1 and 2 Foreign Enterprise Service Corporation cross checks	Fines and court action for breaching Labor laws
9	Sign one official and one non-official rental contract with the landlord	As 1 and 2 Checks on the landlord	Possible court action for fraud
10	Not renew all licenses and permits on time	Commercial and Industrial Bureau	Usually OK provided remedial action is taken
11	Not carry out tax filings and other compulsory filings	As 1 and 2 Tax Bureau and Commercial and Industrial Bureau	As 1

2. If you do not officially declare all your expenses through the RO account or have separate funds to finance the local activities, then firstly, you are not in compliance, and secondly, you run the risk of staff turning this against you when they are dismissed or leave the company (blackmailing and threats to disclose malpractices to local authorities are common in order to seek own financial gains). Local staff may even manipulate the company records to ensure it is not in compliance—in order to hold leverage against you in the event of any disciplinary action being taken against them at a later stage. It is relatively common.
3. No government likes tax evasion and China is no exception to the rule. The penalties for late payments, non-payment and other transgressions (naivety is no excuse) can be severe—often up to five times the amount due, plus the original liability. In cases of blatant evasion, businesses can have their licenses withdrawn and assets seized.
4. With an increased number of inter-government bureau cooperations, information sharing activities and checks initiated by individual tip offs, the likelihood of falling into the taxman's hands is high. If you have any doubts, please seek professional advice immediately—this is the one area it is best not to mess about with, fees spent on decent advice are less than the amounts levied in fines and penalties!

4 RO Budget

The following table shows a typical budget for an RO in China, and gives you some idea of the costs and issues you will need to consider:

Representative Office in Shenzhen monthly expenses forecast sheet

	Running expense	Notes	Amount RMB eqv.
1	Office rental and management fee		10,000.00
2	Salary for chief representative		24,300.00
3	Salary for two local employees (RMB4,000 and RMB10,000)	1	14,000.00
4	FESCO Fee and social insurance for two local employees		3,444.03
	including: FESCO fee	2	1,500.00
	pension insurance		1,048.77
	medical insurance		815.71
	injury insurance		58.27
	unemployment insurance		21.28
5	Other miscellaneous (i.e., telephone, office utilities, etc.)	3	6,000.00
6	Bank charges		

(continued)

(continued)

	Running expense	Notes	Amount RMB eqv.
7	Stamp duty		
8	Individual Income Tax	4	5,988.99
	including for Chief Representative		4,666.67
	for local employees		1,322.32
9	Driver	5	
10	Apartment rental	5	
	Total monthly running expense		63,733.01

Corporate Income Tax and Business Tax (monthly)

	RMB	
Corporate Income Tax	1,874.50	(63,733.01/ 85%*10%*25%)
Business Tax	3,749.00	(63,733.01/85%*5%)
Total Corporate Income Tax and Business Tax to pay	5,623.50	

Notes (1) Based on our assumption that two local Chinese staff will be hired with the monthly salary of RMB4,000 and 10,000 net, respectively; (2) FESCO fee is paid to the Foreign Enterprise Service Company at RMB750 per capita per month for local Chinese staff. The RO shall also cover employees' welfare, normally including pension, medical, unemployment and injury; (3) based on the assumption that a normal situation is faced; (4) based on the assumption that the RO bears the IIT expense. Alternatively, the RO can choose the arrangement that employees bear the IIT expense; (5) some of the boxes have been left blank for your own calculations and budget

Other Issues

1 Intellectual Property

Intellectual property has always been a big concern for foreign investors in China. Since the enforcement of IP laws is not so satisfactory at present, it is therefore very important for foreign investors to know how to protect their intellectual property before any infringement occurs.

Trademarks

Patent infringement is becoming more and more common, and combatting this is a major challenge for foreign companies. When you come to China, you need to consider how to ensure your competitors will not pirate your key technologies. Patent application will be the first step. Careful drafting of the application will help your patent to be approved by the patent authority without too many changes, so you can enjoy the broadest protection allowed by law. In many patent lawsuits, the patentee loses the case simply because of bad wording of the claims. Therefore, it is very important to find a reliable professional firm to take care of your patent application.

Patents are further classified into inventions, utilities models and designs under Chinese Patent Law. The official fees for patent application will vary depending on the specific application and the category, for both the initial registration and renewal. Invention patents are for 20 years, and a utility model or design for 10 years. Unlike trademarks, once the period of validity of a patent expires, it cannot be renewed.

Domain Names

With the rapid expansion of the Internet, more and more people have realized the importance of domain names. Usually, a company will register its trademark or its enterprise name as its domain name, and a good domain name ending ".cn" will be very useful for marketing. Domain name registration follows the principle of "first come, first served." It is very important to register the trademark/enterprise name before it is hijacked by others. A simple search of your company name or trademark on the Internet will show the importance of a domain name. The annual fees for registering such a domain name are very low.

Trade Secrets

"Trade secrets" is a very broad concept, and it may include all the information and documents that will bring economic benefits to the company and that should be protected by the company—this will include client information, price, design, production methods and procedures, programmes, etc. Trade secrets should not only be protected from competitors, but also from key personnel of the company.

Once your company is in the position of negotiation (e.g. for joint venture setup or an OEM contract) with another party and you need to disclose some of your trade secrets, be sure to sign a confidentiality agreement with the other parties and clearly let them know that you are sharing trade secrets.

For key personnel in charge of your trade secrets, a confidentiality agreement and sometimes also a non-competition agreement are also recommended. However, since non-competition agreements also fall within the scope of labor law, it is very important for the company to make sure that all the clauses in the non-competition agreement are in compliance with employment laws.

IP Management System

Intellectual property protection is very professional and complicated work. We suggest company should have personnel in charge of its IP related matters, building and keeping files, coordinating with external IP counsels, monitoring of the IP status, etc.

It will also be helpful to educate your employees to improve their IP consciousness, especially the sales people who are most familiar with the market and the distribution of fake products. Good communication with your clients will also help you to find clues on infringement.

2 Upgrading Your Representative Office

With so many changes in market development in China, and a lot of jockeying for position amongst international companies wanting a slice of the action, an increasing number of companies are finding that they need to change their structures. This might involve either upgrading their existing China operations, merging them or housing different entities under one controlling China venture in order to become more effective and efficient. This section looks at a variety of different scenarios and how you can best merge, re-structure or re-locate these businesses to suit the needs of your China operations for the next few years.

ROs are not permitted to trade, so this brings restrictions that may not now be pertinent given China's accession to the WTO and its own market liberalization. What you need and how to go about it depends very much on what it is you want to do—but let's assume that you need to import or export under your own steam or you need to sell services. How to upgrade your existing RO?

Almost certainly this will require a new incorporation in China—either a Wholly Foreign-Owned Enterprise (WFOE), or, if it's in a currently restricted industry, a Joint Venture. Here it's worthwhile looking at when certain activities are to be relaxed in accordance with WTO implementation. Foreign companies can now set up wholly owned distribution companies called Foreign Invested Commercial Enterprises. This may affect what you can set up so you need to discuss this fully with your consultant beforehand.

Without doubt, a wise investor will also take into consideration the fact that WTO agenda and actual implementation are sometimes moving along at different speeds. Please do not be so concentrated on the new dates put forward by the government. Instead do your homework, talking not only to the approval authorities but also to the other departments like customs or tax bureau to confirm that what has been deployed from Beijing is actually implemented locally.

However, back to the RO upgrade. Essentially, having decided whether or not you need to set up a JV or WFOE to provide you with sales or service abilities and/ or import–export rights, you have the choice then either to close the RO, to keep it going, or to close it and replace it with a local branch of your existing WFOE or JV.

If you want to close the RO, a tax audit is required and it is normally the time during which all previous or inherited wrongdoings come to the surface. As a result, it is important to keep bookkeeping and operations in line with regulations, so that when it comes to close the RO no problems shall affect your new China plans.

So if needing to sell, or import–export, you need to set up a WFOE or JV and either close the RO entirely, or replace it with a sub-branch of the new entity. Closure of RO can be affected at the same time as establishing your new trading entity.

Relocating Your RO

If an RO changes the name of its office, the names or number of its representatives, the scope of its business, its duration, or its address, it must apply to the local State Administration for Industry and Commerce (SAIC) Bureau for approval of such changes by submitting related documents.

Changing the Chief Representative

If a new representative is to be appointed (or the address of the RO changed), a power of attorney or authorization letter issued by the parent enterprise along with the identity certificate of the new representative, notarized by the local notary public office and authenticated by the Chinese embassy/consulate, must be submitted in addition to the new representative's resume and other required documents when applying for approval of the change must be submitted in addition to the new representative's resume and other required documents when applying for approval of the change.

The detailed process varies depending on location. In Beijing, the following process must be gone through:

- Final IIT clearance from local tax bureau for the outgoing chief representative.
- New chief representative needs a new working card.
- Business license must be changed to the name of new chief representative.
- Registration with local and state tax bureaus must be amended.
- Enterprise code must be changed to reflect new chief representative.
- Public Security Bureau record changed for new chief representative.
- Resident card and Z visa obtained for new chief representative.

In Shanghai, a similar process is required, along with changes to relevant documentation with the statistics bureau, customs and the ROs bank.

In Shenzhen, again a similar process is needed, as well as change of documentation with the finance bureau.

Summary

Re-structuring your China operations is a process that requires a fair amount of planning, understanding, and local expertise. However, it's not as difficult and complex as many assume it to be. But administratively, it is awkward, and of course there are numerous tax and legal considerations when establishing operations and developing new ones. The sensible practical application of China's foreign investment law, rather than legal theory, will generally get you where you want to be.

3 Closing Down a Representative Office

It may happen that due to the company's development abroad or in the PRC, the RO structure does not suit the needs of the investor any longer and must be altered accordingly.

Here are a few examples of instances in which an RO may not suit your requirements any longer:

- The holding company has closed down or changed business activities.
- You may want to wind down the RO activities.
- The RO has not been operating in compliance to its business scope or the local regulations and you may want to re-start on a "clean sheet."
- The current location needs upgrading in term of bigger/smaller space or different office and you want to close it at the same time.
- You need a local RMB billing entity.
- The current RO business scope does not suit your requirements any longer.
- You need to upgrade your China structure/entity.

As a general rule of thumb, when you require restructuring your operations in the PRC, it is normally the time when all previous wrongdoings or malpractices come to the surface and must be dealt with in order to move to the next step.

Closing down an RO is no exception, as a closing audit must be performed by the tax bureau before you are allowed to start the procedure. As long as the RO has no overdue taxes or other issues to be reported to the authorities, then the de-registration procedure can begin.

Firstly, applications shall be made at the tax bureaus (both local and national) with related papers and RO closure resolution of the parent company, with the director's signature and parent company's chop. In most of the cases the following documents need to be provided:

- an audit report up to the current month RO tax returns ledgers and vouchers;
- tax registration certificates (original and copy with RO chops);
- if the RO is not subject to taxation then a tax exempt notice from the tax bureau confirming this status has to be presented.

Secondly, cancel the bank accounts, cheque book, signature card, then withdraw the remaining funds or remit them back to the holding company. A proof of bank account cancellation should be issued by the bank in this step.

The third step is to obtain the approval certificate from customs together with a declaration on the reasons behind the decision to wind up operations in China (the same written explanations shall be given to all other bureaus involved in the closing procedures). This is required in order to clear up all records at customs involving any office equipment, car or samples imports. (Note: the proofs of tax registration and bank account cancellation must be shown to the customs.)

The fourth step is the cancellation of the business license. In order to do so, all the previous approvals notices from state and local tax bureaus, the bank and customs should be shown to the Industrial and Commercial Bureau together with a board resolution from the holding company.

The fifth step is to cancel the legal code certificate of the RO.

The final step is the cancellation of the chops with the Public Security Bureau.

Normally such applications take around 6–9 months depending on the level of cooperation between the company representative and the different bureaus involved and the extent of the closing audit required by the tax bureau. It should be noted that the parent enterprise of the RO will be held responsible for any unsettled matters of its RO.

Glossary of Terms

AIC	Administration of Industry and Commerce
BOFTEC	Bureau of Foreign Trade and Economic Co-operation (local approvals authority)
CIT	Corporate Income Tax
CJV	Co-operative Joint Venture
DTA	Double Tax Agreement
EDR	Exemption, deduction and refund (for VAT)
EJV	Equity Joint Venture
EPZ	Export Processing Zone (state level)
ETDZ	Economic and Technological Development Zone (state level)
FDI	Foreign Direct Investment
FICE	Foreign Invested Commercial Enterprise
FIE	Foreign Invested Enterprise
FTZ	Free Trade Zone (state level)
GAC	General Administration of Customs
HIDZ	Hi-Tech Industrial Development Zone (state level)
IIT	Individual Income Tax
JV	Joint Venture
LLJG	lai liao jia gong/Processing Factory (processing with supplied materials by foreign party)
M&A	Merger and Acquisition

MOC	Ministry of Commerce
MOF	Ministry of Finance
MRA	Maximum Refundable Amount
NDRC	National Development and Reform Commission
PRC	People's Republic of China
RMB	Renminbi (Chinese currency unit, also know as Yuan or, colloquially, "kuai")
RO	Representative Office
SAFE	State Administration of Foreign Exchange
SAIC	State Administration of Industry and Commerce
SAT	State Administration of Taxation
SDPC	State Development and Planning Commission
SETC	State Economic and Trade Commission
SEZ	Special Economic Zone (state level)
VAT	Value Added Tax
WFOE	Wholly Foreign Owned Enterprise (known colloquially as Woofies")
WTO	World Trade Organisation

DEZAN SHIRA & ASSOCIATES

Corporate Establishment, Tax, Accounting & Payroll Throughout Asia

China's Premier Foreign Direct Investment Practice

Providing business advisory, corporate establishment, tax, accounting, payroll, due diligence and audit services to multinational investors and SMEs in China since 1992.

Please contact our offices below or e-mail info@dezshira.com.

Beijing Office:
Sabrina Zhang
Regional Partner
beijing@dezshira.com
+86 10 6566 0088

Dalian Office:
Adam Livermore
Regional Manager
dalian@dezshira.com
+86 411 6299 0101

Qingdao Office:
Liming Zhang
Senior Associate
qingdao@dezshira.com
+86 532 6677 5461

Tianjin Office:
Richard Hoffmann
Manager
tianjin@dezshira.com

Shanghai Office:
Olaf Griese
Partner
shanghai@dezshira.com
+86 21 6358 8686

Hangzhou Office:
Helen Ye
Manager
hangzhou@dezshira.com
+86 571 5685 9956

Ningbo Office:
Lily Wang
Manager
ningbo@dezshira.com
+86 574 8733 8682

Suzhou Office
Fabian Knopf
Business Development Associate
suzhou@dezshira.com

Guangzhou Office:
Rosario DiMaggio
Manager
guangzhou@dezshira.com
+86 20 3825 1725

Zhongshan Office:
Lisa Qian
Manager
zhongshan@dezshira.com
+86 760 8826 9592

Shenzhen Office:
Alberto Vettoretti
Managing Partner
shenzhen@dezshira.com
+86 755 8366 4120

Hong Kong Office:
Joe Sze
Manager
hongkong@dezshira.com
+852 2376 0334

Also in India and Vietnam

 india@dezshira.com   vietnam@dezshira.com

www.dezshira.com

Members of The Leading Edge Alliance, the world's second largest accounting association

www.LeadingEdgeAlliance.com